W9-AJO-544

Food and Festivals

ISRAEL

Ronne Randall

WITHDRAWN

RAINTREE
STECK-VAUGHN
PUBLISHERS
A Steck-Vaughn Company

Austin, Texas

Food and Festivals

ISRAEL

Other titles:

The Caribbean • China • India
Mexico • West Africa

Cover photograph: A kibbutz worker with boxes of juicy strawberries

Title page: Children with freshly picked olives in an olive grove

Contents page: A Jewish man blows a ram's horn to mark the festival of Rosh Hashanah.

© Copyright 1999, text, Steck-Vaughn Company

All rights reserved. No part of this book may be reproduced or utilized in any form or by any means, electronic or mechanical, including photocopying, recording, or by any information storage and retrieval system, without permission in writing from the Publisher. Inquiries should be addressed to: Copyright Permissions, Steck-Vaughn Company, P.O. Box 26015, Austin, TX 78755.

Published by Raintree Steck-Vaughn Publishers, an imprint of Steck-Vaughn Company

Printed in Italy. Bound in the United States.
1 2 3 4 5 6 7 8 9 0 03 02 01 00 99

Library of Congress Cataloging-in-Publication Data
Randall, Ronne.
Israel / Ronne Randall.
    p.   cm.—(Food and festivals)
Includes bibliographical references and index.
Summary: Describes how different kinds of food common in various regions of Israel are grown and prepared and the part foods play during Passover, Rosh Hashanah, Hanukkah, and a Bar Mitzvah.
ISBN 0-8172-5759-4 (hard)
ISBN 0-7398-0959-8 (soft)
1. Cookery, Jewish—Juvenile literature.
2. Holiday cookery—Isarel—Juvenile literature.
3. Israel—Social life and customs—Juvenile literature.
[1. Cookery, Jewish. 2. Food habits—Israel.
3. Food habits—Israel. 4. Israel—Social life and customs]
I. Title. II. Series.
TX724.R36   1999
641.5'676—dc21   98-45756

CONTENTS

Israel and Its Food

ISRAEL

Israel's place in the world

LEBANON

SYRIA

Sea of Galilee

MEDITERRANEAN SEA

Tel Aviv
Jaffa

Jordan

JORDAN

Jerusalem
Bethlehem

Dead Sea

ISRAEL

N

Negev Desert

EGYPT

| 0 | 100 km |
| 0 | 50 miles |

Areas where government is shared
between Israelis and Palestinians

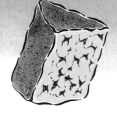

FRUIT

Many different citrus fruits grow in Israel, such as grapefruit and the famous Jaffa oranges. Olives have grown in Israel for thousands of years

VEGETABLES

Most Israelis eat lots of salads, made with vegetables such as tomatoes, peppers, and onions. Potatoes are used to make dishes such as *latkes* (potato pancakes).

GRAINS AND PULSES

These include wheat, sunflower seeds, and chickpeas. Chickpeas are used to make *falafel*, which is so popular it is Israel's "national food."

POULTRY

Most people in Israel are Jews or Muslims, whose religions do not allow them to eat pork. Chicken or turkey is used in most meat dishes.

DAIRY FOODS

Butter and cheeses, like the goat's cheese in this picture, are made from the milk of cows, sheep, and goats.

HONEY

Beehives in Israel produce tons of honey every year. Honey cakes, like the one shown here, are eaten on Rosh Hashanah.

Food and Farming

Israel is a small country on the eastern coast of the Mediterranean Sea. It is bordered by Jordan, Syria, Lebanon, and Egypt. Much of the land is dry and rocky, but irrigation systems bring water to desert areas.

Jews and Arabs have lived in this area of the Middle East for thousands of years. In 1948, the modern state of Israel was created as a Jewish homeland, so today most people who live in Israel are Jewish. Food is an important part of Jewish life, and no festival or celebration is complete without a special meal and traditional treats.

◀ This Arab family has been picking olives. Olive trees grow well in the drier parts of Israel.

Fruits and vegetables

Apples, peaches, pears, plums... many kinds of fruit grow in Israel's warm, sunny climate. Sweet, juicy oranges from groves near the port of Jaffa are world-famous. Olives, figs, and grapes grow in the hilly northern region known as the Galilee.

Many farms in Israel are kibbutzim, where groups of people live and work together. Farmers produce large crops of tomatoes, peppers, onions, cucumbers, and potatoes. Vegetables like these are used in salads, which are an important part of most Israeli meals—even breakfast.

◄ Juicy strawberries are just one of the many fruits grown in Israel.

7

Meat

KOSHER FOOD

"Kosher" comes from a Hebrew word meaning "correct." The laws explaining which foods are kosher come from the Torah, the Jewish holy book. All fruits, vegetables, and grains are kosher. Many types of fish are kosher, too, but meat must come only from certain animals and birds.

The main religion in Israel is Judaism, which has strict food laws forbidding any meat that comes from pigs. Islam, the second most widespread religion, also forbids pig meat. Most beef comes from abroad and is quite expensive, so chicken and turkey make a very important part of many dishes. Breaded turkey steaks called *schnitzels* are popular everyday food. Israelis eat more poultry per person than anyone else in the world.

These children are ▶ collecting eggs from chickens. Poultry farms also supply most of the meat eaten in Israel.

▲ A shepherd looks after his goats near Bethlehem.

Dairy foods

Milk, butter, and cheese come from Holstein cows, which are raised on pastureland in the north of Israel. Many Bedouin Arabs who live in the desert raise goats and sheep, which also provide lots of milk and cheese.

This Bedouin girl is ▶ shaping cheeses made from goat's milk.

▲ A Bedouin woman preparing dough for pita bread. Pita is a traditional Arab bread, which is now popular with everyone in Israel.

Grains, seeds, and pulses

Wheat is mainly used to make bread. It is grown in the dry southern regions of Israel. Sunflower seeds, sesame seeds, and peanuts are used in cooking and to make oil. Pulses such as chickpeas are a basic ingredient of many everyday foods.

Many peoples, many foods

Jews from all over the world have come to live in Israel, bringing with them a variety of traditions and ways of cooking food. These have blended with the foods and traditions of their Arab neighbors. *Falafel* is an Arab dish that has become so popular it is considered Israel's national food. It is a spicy, deep-fried chickpea patty, usually eaten in pita bread with salad and tahini sauce. You can buy it as a snack from street-corner stands in every Israeli town.

A man frying ▶ *falafel* at a food stand on a street in Jerusalem

Passover

Every spring, Jewish people celebrate the weeklong festival of Passover (called Pesach in Hebrew). Passover marks the time, more than 3,000 years ago, when the Jews were freed from slavery in Egypt. Once they were free, they set out on a forty-year journey across the desert to the Promised Land of Israel. Today, many Jews travel from their homes around the world to celebrate Passover in Israel.

HOW DO YOU SAY...?

The *ch* in words such as Pesach, *charoseth*, *challah, and* Chanukah is pronounced like a rough H—as if you were lightly clearing your throat.

▼ People in Jerusalem stock up on food, ready for the Passover celebrations.

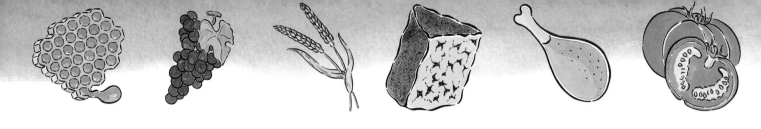

During Passover, Jews do not eat ordinary bread, or any food made with leavening, the ingredient that makes dough rise. Instead, they eat a flat, crackerlike bread called *matzoh*, which is made without leavening. In Israel, many bakeries close for Passover, and it is difficult to find ordinary bread, even in supermarkets.

MATZOH

Jews eat *matzoh* at Passover to remind them of their escape from slavery. When the Jews fled from Egypt, they had no time to bake bread for their long journey across the desert. So they put the dough on their backs, where the sun baked it hard and flat.

▼ Baking *matzoh* for Passover in a traditional bakery in Jerusalem

Preparing for Passover

In the days leading up to Passover, Jewish families clean their homes thoroughly and put away any food containing leavening. During the festival week, they eat only foods that are "kosher for Passover."

Like all Jewish festivals, Passover begins at sundown on the evening before the first full day of the festival. On that evening there is a big, festive meal called a Seder.

▼ A Jewish man prepares for Passover by cleaning his cooking equipment in a tub of boiling water.

▲ The whole family gets together to share the Seder. The big golden goblet in the middle of the table is Elijah's cup.

The Seder

During the Seder, the story of the escape from Egypt is read from a book called the Haggadah. Songs are sung, and special foods are served. The Seder may go on for many hours, but it must finish by midnight.

ELIJAH'S CUP

Adults drink wine and children drink grape juice at the Seder. It is the custom to put a special cup of wine on the table for the prophet Elijah, who is said to visit every Jewish home on the first night of Passover.

THE SEDER PLATE

Some foods are served on a decorated plate called the Seder plate, and they have symbolic meanings. There is a green vegetable, for new life and growth, and a bitter herb (usually horseradish) to represent the bitterness of slavery. *Charoseth* symbolizes the mortar Jewish slaves used when they built cities in Egypt. Roasted egg and bone symbolize the lamb that was sacrificed at Passover in ancient times.

Food for the Seder

It is traditional to begin the Seder with boiled eggs. These are served in saltwater, to symbolize the tears shed by the Jews when they were slaves in Egypt. People also eat chicken soup and roasted meat, usually lamb or chicken. *Charoseth* is a delicious, sweet paste that is eaten with *matzoh*. There is a recipe for *charoseth* on the opposite page.

▼ The pictures and Hebrew words that decorate this Seder plate help tell the story of Passover. The middle bowl on the left contains *charoseth*.

Charoseth

EQUIPMENT

Knife
Chopping board
Food processor

INGREDIENTS

1 apple, peeled and cored

2½ oz. (75 g) shelled almonds

2 teaspoons of sugar

1 teaspoon of cinnamon

3 Tablespoons of red grape juice

If you don't have a food processor, grate the apple and chop the nuts into small pieces.

1 Chop the apple into chunks.

2 Put the apple and almonds into the food processor. Blend together until they are in small pieces.

3 Add the sugar, cinnamon, and grape juice and blend the mixture into a thick paste.

4 To serve, spread the paste thickly on plain crackers.

Be careful when using sharp knives. Ask an adult to help you.

17

A Bar Mitzvah

A Jewish boy's thirteenth birthday is very special. This is when he becomes a bar mitzvah, or "son of the commandment." In Jewish law, he is now considered a man.

Saturday is the Jewish Sabbath, and on the Saturday nearest the boy's birthday a bar mitzvah ceremony is held in the synagogue. The boy is called forward to read from the Torah scroll for the first time. He wears his prayer shawl, called a *tallith*, for the very first time, too. After this, he will wear the *tallith* at every Sabbath service.

▼ This boy is celebrating his bar mitzvah at the Western Wall, a Jewish holy place in Jerusalem. He is wearing his *tallith* over his head.

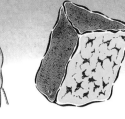

A bar mitzvah party

After the ceremony in the synagogue, there is a party to celebrate the boy's coming of age. Family and friends gather to rejoice together, and there is music, dancing, and a festive meal.

▼ Crunchy, colorful vegetables are used to make delicious salads like this one.

When a bar mitzvah party is held on a kibbutz, the meal is usually set out on long tables, and people help themselves to a delicious combination of foods. Many of the dishes are made with freshly picked vegetables grown on the kibbutz. There is a recipe for an Israeli vegetable salad on page 20.

Israeli Vegetable Salad

EQUIPMENT

Knife
Chopping board
Grater
Deep bowl
Small pitcher (for mixing dressing)
Fork

INGREDIENTS

$1/2$ head of lettuce
2 medium tomatoes
$1/2$ cucumber, peeled
5 radishes
6 scallions
1 green pepper
1 carrot

3 Tablespoons of olive oil
2 Tablespoons of lemon juice
Pinch of salt and pepper
2 Tablespoons of fresh parsley, chopped

Chop all the vegetables except the carrot into small cubes and put them in the deep bowl.

Grate the carrot and mix it with the other vegetables.

Just before serving, put the lemon juice, oil, salt, and pepper into a small pitcher and mix with a fork.

Pour the dressing over the salad and mix well. Sprinkle the parsley on top.

Be careful when using sharp knives. Ask an adult to help you.

Bat mitzvahs

A Jewish girl becomes a bat mitzvah, or "daughter of the commandment," when she is 12 or 13 years old. The exact time when the ceremony is held depends on the traditions of her family and community. Some Jewish people do not have bat mitzvah ceremonies.

THE TORAH

The Torah scroll read in the synagogue is handwritten on parchment. The ancient Hebrew words are written so slowly and carefully by a holy scribe (called a *sofer*) that it can take years to complete one scroll.

▼ A rabbi helps a young girl practice reading the Torah scroll.

Rosh Hashanah

Rosh Hashanah, the Jewish New Year, is celebrated in late summer. According to tradition, it is the anniversary of the day when God finished creating the world. It marks the start of a ten-day period when Jews think about the year gone by and promise to make a fresh start in the year to come.

ROUND *CHALLAH*

The traditional bread called *challah* is usually baked as a long, braided loaf, but on Rosh Hashanah it is round. This symbolizes the cycle of the year and also hope for a year unbroken by sadness.

A family ▶ enjoys a meal together on Rosh Hashanah. There is a round *challah* and fruit dipped in honey on the table.

THE *SHOFAR*

The *shofar* is an ancient instrument—it is mentioned in the Bible. On Rosh Hashanah, it is used to blow four special notes, each with a different meaning. The first note calls people to attention, the second calls them together, the third represents hope, and the fourth welcomes the new year.

On Rosh Hashanah everyone goes to the synagogue to pray for a good year. There, a ram's horn called the *shofar* is blown, as a kind of "wake-up" call to remind people of their promises to God. As they return home, people greet one another with the Hebrew words *"L'shanah tovah!"*—"A good year!"

▼ A man blowing a *shofar* during the New Year prayers

A sweet year

Jews celebrate the New Year with foods made with honey, to show that they hope for a "sweet" year. The main New Year's meal begins with a blessing over *challah*, a traditional bread eaten on the Sabbath and during festivals. Dishes include slices of *challah* and slices of apple dipped in honey. The meal finishes with a sweet, golden, honey cake. There is a recipe for a honey cake on the opposite page.

◀ Every New Year's meal includes sweet foods like this honey cake.

New Year's Honey Cake

EQUIPMENT

Sieve

Large mixing bowl

Medium bowl

Electric mixer or wooden spoon

Teakettle

Measuring cup

2-lb loaf pan, greased and lined with foil

INGREDIENTS

$1/3$ cup (50 g) self-rising flour

$1/3$ cup (50 g) all-purpose flour

$1/4$ teaspoon of baking soda

$1/2$ teaspoon of nutmeg

$1/2$ teaspoon of cinnamon

1 Tablespoon of cocoa powder

1 medium egg

$1/2$ cup (100 g) sugar

$1/3$ cup (75 ml) cooking oil

$1/3$ cup (125 g) honey

$1/3$ cup (120 ml) boiling water

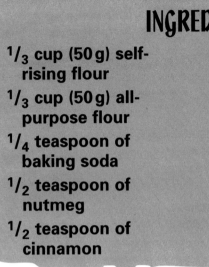

①

Put the flour, baking soda, cocoa, and spices into a sieve over the large mixing bowl and shake them gently through the sieve.

②

In the medium bowl, mix the egg with the sugar. Add the oil and honey and mix together.

③

Add the egg mixture to the flour mixture, pour in the boiling water and mix everything together until smooth.

④

Pour the mixture into the greased and lined pan, and bake for 45 minutes at 375° F (190° C). Leave the cake to cool in the pan before turning out and serving.

Be careful when using a hot oven. Ask an adult to help you.

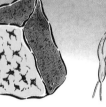

Hanukkah

At Hanukkah, Jews light the candles in a special candle holder called a *menorah*. Every night for eight nights, they light one more candle, using a "helper" candle called a *shammes*. On the eighth night, all the candles are burning brightly, lighting up the dark winter night. Jewish people do this in memory of events that took place more than 2,000 years ago.

▼ A family gathers around the *menorah* to sing blessings and light the candles for the last night of Hanukkah.

At that time, the Jews were ruled by a king who would not allow them to worship God. Instead, he made them bow down to statues. But some Jews refused to obey him, and eventually they defeated the king's soldiers and took control of the Temple in Jerusalem. When they wanted to light the holy lamp, called the *menorah*, they had only enough oil to last one day. But, according to legend, a miracle happened, and the oil lasted for eight days and nights.

▼ Foil-covered chocolate coins are often used as prizes in the *dreidel* game.

THE *DREIDEL* GAME

For centuries, Jewish children have played the *dreidel* game at Hanukkah. The *dreidel* is a spinning top decorated with four Hebrew letters. A few coins or pieces of candy are put on the table, and each player tries to win them by spinning the *dreidel*.

Hanukkah treats

CHEESE AT HANUKKAH

In some families it is traditional to eat cheese dishes at Hanukkah, in honor of Judith, a brave Jewish woman who fed lots of cheese to an enemy general. This made him thirsty, so he drank a great deal of wine. When he was drunk and sleepy, Judith cut off his head!

Throughout the eight days of Hanukkah, people give each other presents, and there are parties, games, and special foods to enjoy. Foods cooked in oil are traditional at Hanukkah, as a reminder of the miracle of the oil. In Israel, the most popular Hanukkah foods are sugary doughnuts called *sufganiyot* and potato pancakes called *latkes*.

Doughnuts and potato *latkes* for Hanukkah ▼

Potato *Latkes*

EQUIPMENT

Food processor	Frying pan
Sieve	Large spoon
Mixing bowl	Spatula
Wooden spoon	Paper towel

INGREDIENTS

3 medium potatoes, peeled and cut into chunks

1 medium onion

4 Tablespoons of all-purpose flour

1 large egg, beaten

Salt and pepper to taste

Vegetable oil for frying

If you don't have a food processor, use a grater to grate the potatoes and onion.

1 Put the potatoes and onion in the food processor and process them until fine.

2 Put the mixture in a sieve, squeeze out the excess liquid and throw the liquid away.

3 Put the mixture in a bowl and add all the remaining ingredients except the oil. Beat them together to make a thick batter.

4 Pour about 1/4 in. (1 cm) of oil into a frying pan and heat it. When the oil is hot, drop in large spoonfuls of batter and fry them until golden brown. Drain on paper towel and serve.

Be careful when frying. Ask an adult to help you.

Glossary

Arabs   A group of people who come from North Africa and the area between the east coast of the Mediterranean Sea and Iran.

Homeland   A country that is special to a group of people. They think of this land as their home even if they were not born there.

Irrigation systems   Underground pipes that carry rainwater or seawater to farms in areas that get very little rain.

Jews   Followers of a religion called Judaism. Jews believe in one God and live by the laws set down in the Torah, the first five books of the Bible.

Kibbutzim   Farms in Israel where everyone lives and works together. The word for one farm is "kibbutz."

Muslims   Followers of a religion called Islam. Muslims believe in one God, whom they call Allah. They live by laws set down in their holy book, the Koran.

Pulses   The seeds of certain vegetable crops such as peas, beans, and lentils.

Scribe   A religious person who is specially trained to write out the words of the Torah in the ancient Hebrew language.

Scroll   A long roll of paper, cloth or parchment, on which something is written.

Slavery   Being forced to work without payment or reward. Slaves are owned by the people they work for.

Symbolic   When an object stands for something else, it is called symbolic.

Synagogue   A building where Jews come together to pray and learn.

Temple   The very first synagogue, built in Jerusalem about 3,000 years ago. The Western Wall of the Temple is still standing and it is an important holy place for Jews today.

Photograph and artwork acknowledgments
The publishers would like to thank the following for contributing to the pictures in this book:
ASAP 15/Richard Nowitz, 18/Richard Nowitz, 19/Cathy Raff; Antony Blake 5 (bottom right)/Trevor Wood, 24/Trevor Wood; Ffotograff 9 (top)/Patricia Aitchie; Robert Harding 26/E. Simanor, 28; Impact 11/John Cole; Popperfoto 12/Reuters, 14 (top)/Reuters; Zev Radovan 5 (centre right), 8, 13; Stock Market *contents page*, 5 (bottom left), 9 (bottom) 10, 16, 23, 27; Trip *cover*/A. Tovy, *title page*/A. Tovy, 6/A. Tovy, 7/A. Tovy, 21/H. Rogers; Wayland Picture Library 5 (top left), 5 (top right), 5 (centre left). Fruit and vegetable artwork is by Tina Barber. Map artwork on page 4 is by Peter Bull and Hardlines. Step-by-step recipe artwork is by Judy Stevens.

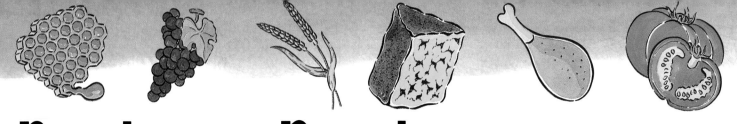

Books to Read

Bracken, Thomas. *Good Luck Symbols and Talismans*. New York: Chelsea House, 1997.

Clark, Anne, et al. *Hanukkah* (World of Holidays). Austin, TX: Raintree Steck-Vaughn, 1998.

Haskins, James. *Count Your Way Through Israel*. New York: First Avenue Editions, 1992.

Patterson, Jose and Patrick Burke. *Israel* (Country Fact Files). Austin, TX: Raintree Steck-Vaughn, 1997.

Silverman, Maida. *Israel: The Founding of a Modern Nation*. New York: Dial Books for Young Readers, 1998.

Slim, Hugo. *A Feast of Festivals*. New York: HarperCollins, 1996.

Waldman, Neil. *The Golden City: Jerusalem's 3,000 Years*. New York: Atheneum, 1995.

——. *Masada*. New York: Morrow Junior Books, 1998.

Index

Page numbers in **bold** mean there is a photograph on the page.

© Copyright 1998 Wayland (Publishers) Ltd.